Through The Red Door's Open Maw

Poems
Jessica June Cato

Beyond The Veil Press

Poems © 2023 Jessica June Cato
Manuscript © 2023 Beyond The Veil Press
Cover Art © 2023 Danielle Mitchell

Created on the lands of the Ute, Arapahoe, and Cheyenne peoples, in the so-called United States of America.

ISBN: 9798854332941

TABLE OF CONTENTS

INTRODUCTION

Jessica Cato's chapbook, *Through the Red Door's Open Maw*, invites readers through the threshold into a liminal place where a hellish past blurs with present-day suburbia. These poems are a reckoning with the residual guilt and self-perception that haunts the bones—lineage, familial abandonment, addiction, mental illness, and queerphobia traced back to that red door, the open maw.

Cato reflects on love as foreign—comparing ancestries as if checking the past to see if there is anything innate in her familial bones, makeup, or core. In the poem, *I'm Afraid Of Nice Kitchen Knives*, she writes, *"Is this what it's like to hold me? Something so sharp and grave?/How do you let your guard down around something like that?"*

Through the Red Door's Open Maw is a naked and honest reflection about what remains of one's past self and how to break free from beliefs of what is intrinsic to selfhood, to live beyond into goodness that need not be compared with personal history; instead, can shine all on its own.

—Matthew Feinstein, author of *Breeds of Breath*

CONTENT WARNINGS

This chapbook contains work that mentions death, drug use, and alcoholism. Please read carefully.

United States
Suicide and Mental Health Crisis Line: 988
Suicide Prevention Line: 1.800.273.8255
Sexual Assault Hotline: 1.800.656.4673
Domestic Violence Hotline: 1.800.799.7233
Substance Abuse Hotline: 1.800.662.4357
Self-Harm Textline: Text "Connect" to 741741
Trans Lifeline: 1-877-565-8860
The Trevor Project: 1-866-488-7386 or Text: 678-678

Canada
Trans Lifeline (CA): 1-877-330-6366
Talk Suicide Canada: 1-833-456-4566
Quebec residents: 1-866-277-3553 or visit *suicide.ca*
Wellness Together: 1-866-585-0445 or text WELLNESS to 741741
Hope For Wellness (First Peoples, Inuit, and Métis Peoples):
    1-855-242-3310 or connect to online chat: *hopeforwellness.ca*

United Kingdom
Samaritans 116 123

Australia
Lifeline Australia 13 11 14
Beyond Blue 1300 22 4636

More resources at the back of this book and on our website:
beyondtheveilpress.com.

"Home is what you take with you, not what you leave behind."
—N.K. Jemisin, The Fifth Season

For Love, I am so happy to know your heart.

Through The Red Door's Open Maw

Poems
Jessica June Cato

Beyond The Veil Press

CIRCLES ARE SACRED

People put so much faith in circles
Load invaluable cargo onto trucks
Airplane wheels catch us all on the runway
Circular wires to keep connected
Tubes open airways and veins
Allow in oxygen, water, and medicine
Cul-de-sacs protect kids from fast cars
Water wheels churn
Fan blades spin off the coasts in the deserts
to reheat morning coffee
Ocean waves curl and return surfboards to shore
Fireworks bloom in dandelion circles
Streetlights flash green yellow   red
Planets out there and beneath our feet
Pearls curated by the seafloor
Beaded together and precious
Cylinders of ink for love letters
Tree trunks and flower stems
Divinities of circles
So don't feel ashamed when you
Wander around in them

I. BONES AND GRAVE WAX

DISSOCIATION AT 70 MPH

I had no home in my flesh, so I ran
In the car, the freeway lights and I strobed in and out

I came to find the word was dissociation,
That is beside the point

I remember fear, my mortality
whispered in my ear
from the bed it made of my shoulder

It was always close, so I ran
In the car, lamps flashed above the 5

Before the toll roads, after the gentrification
I floated away. Couldn't drift anywhere safe,

a child with no blueprint, a learning echo
I would meander to the farthest edges,
the bedrock of my being

In retrospect, I felt far because I was
We are so much closer to infinity as children

How am I alive?
And what does it mean to be?
If I am here and my mind is elsewhere,
Which where am I?

All the way home

WAS I YOUR DREAM?

Not some sloppy Freudian bullshit
not the teeth falling out, descending
forever, naked in front of an audience dream

More like your dream victim

The way a polar bear dreams of slow seals
and fish without sense or how a falcon
doesn't care it also owns hollow bones
when it dreams of diving
on a pigeon or crane

There were days I couldn't reach three deep breaths
I bet you could see it
Sometimes I scream and it feels
like breaking

I hate it

She and I don't dream of fancy things
We grow like weeds, sneak up the sides of cement
dreaming of the day someone sees us
and lets us be

RICOCHET

There are times the missing you becomes a hole in my chest that burns like your liquor / sweetened memories, a splash of cranberry / The night I showed up with all my things shoved in a tiny hatchback / I ricocheted / Met you in the grocery parking lot, little car packed to the brim / Trash bags pressed tight against the glass / When you saw there was no room for you / sighed and smiled / *I'll meet you there* / You smelled like vodka then, too / In my free fall, your home became ours / Neither quiet nor peaceful, it was there / In that it, we had each other / Before it backfired / Vodka cranberries took you again / Leaving me to keep falling on my own

HERE'S TO MY BODY

What it has done to protect me. My mercurial hands that reminded mother of Nana. Earthen eyes so dark they bleed into my irises. Skin stretched, hips widened with hard work and magic. Neck stiff from worrying over words. Memory sharp, with the smells of summers on T street. Beach melting ice cream, taste of saltwater after sandy hot dogs and french fries. Vacations up north, falling through the snow after my powderpuff sister. So why are some years blotted away? Runny ink to keep me safe. Wax sealed. Vaulted.

HELL CAN BE ANYONE

You are not a monster
She repeats with a hammer
For a tongue.

While claws drag close by
Crack in the floor. Crack in the wall.
Tartarus' open maw. She brings it with her

Perched vulture on the gates of hell
Wonders why it can't stop seeing monsters
While it waits for carcasses to drop.

You are not a monster
To a shattered mirror.

USING A SCYTHE, METAPHORICALLY

A shovel could have worked, too. Sewing and growing are honorable and kind
I was handed a venomous tongue, temper and no way out

You default to ruthless
So do I

I stumble on hidden paths, blade blunted
Clear them myself in a haze, in grief

In vexed explosions, my arm is sore
And joy immeasurable, I reach for a whetstone

Each treasure I uncover here is only mine
There are times I will wonder if your bruised conscience knew

You got your way, I never followed
Esplanade of my own making, distance from the discord

Too tired to balance on your serrated edges

I'M AFRAID OF NICE KITCHEN KNIVES

For they have no remorse. They don't hug food the way old, blunted ones do, painstaking and insolvent. Slow going, they give time for reprieve.

Nice, new kitchen knives are not so generous. Quick, sharp. They want you to pay attention, move with confidence. Demand respect for their potential, faith in their performance. Equal parts dangerous and helpful, depending on how you hold them.

Is this what it's like to hold me? Something so sharp and grave? How do you let your guard down around something like that?

.

NANA'S HOUSE

The screen door was metal
slammed heavily

It creaked open with thick coils
at the corner

We were warned not to touch
with little fingers

because the truth held
no mercy

Trace S shaped decorations
mirrored symmetrical

The paint worn toward the bottom
years of small faces

metal-cold
foreheads always waiting

for someone to come home
Curved concrete slabs

cement walkway
steps

I knew the smell of beans
in the pot

where the roosters sat
looking crooked

from a high shelf I gathered
magnets like friends

on the fridge
I knew pieces

of floor that creaked
garage laundry smell

I knew the characters
in novelas

how far back the rocking chair
swayed

They started and ended
with that door

I knew all this
and still

she called me
stranger

TAINTED

We used to pick snapdragons
at grandma's house
Pinch their sunset heads
make a choir in our hands
We shucked corn over buckets
thought of Aunt Janice
Clear blue of her eyes Iowa sky
The same backyard that told me
to be packed by morning
Same second floor that handed me a roll of trash bags
Driveway that asked for my house key back
Patio swing that called me broken
like my mother
Skyline that swore it could pray the gay away
Gazebo that missed me for years after
The same single stained-glass window
that wondered why I stopped
coming to Christmas.

I WONDER IF THE FAMILY THAT BOUGHT GRANDMA'S HOUSE FEELS ITS GHOSTS

Phantom wars in the halls. Generations of little feet patter on the cement outside, trip over the single outdated stair in the entryway. People hated hard there in the name of love. *I love you so much that I hate these queer, funny pieces of you. Why won't they die?* Half-drowned pasts.

MY GRANDFATHER NEVER SAID MUCH TO ME

My grandmother did most of the talking. Loud words, quick hands. He sat in the rocking chair. Stoic. Gargoyle. Immovable as a mountain. Face tanned, etched in worry and hard work. He went to bed early. A weary life. Never said more to me than *Ay, okies.* I think he hated my mother. For bewitching his son. He should have hated the things that kept them together. He should have hated the way his sons treated his daughter. He should have hated the money hole of a motorcycle leaking oil down the cracked driveway. No matter what house I was in, I carried the other through the threshold with me. My father's proud culture, my mother's twisted tongue. The smallest bannerman, always reminding them of who they hated.

HOUSE WITH THE RED DOOR

Standing on the driveway, here again. Treated like I'm not here, again. So small in my feet. Twelve doors and the last one groans, *You've changed.* Stitched up your pieces, resewn your seams. Renovated doormat. Ready to welcome unworthy soles through the big red door again.

VIOLENTLY AWARE

is this how other people feel?
jaws unclenched, trusting golden doodle hearts
soft and careless

my skittish skeleton pinches
too wary of all the ghosts who see me

the world presses down
crushes the air
roots, cord, stem severed
knuckles white from holding

see?
I don't know any other way to hold

HAVING A CUDDLE WITH YOU
Erasure from Frank O'Hara's "Having A Coke With You"

is even more ▮▮▮▮▮▮▮▮▮▮▮▮▮▮▮▮▮▮▮▮▮▮▮▮▮▮▮▮

▮▮▮▮▮ sick ▮▮▮▮▮▮▮▮▮▮▮▮▮▮▮▮▮▮▮▮▮▮▮▮▮▮

partly because ▮▮▮▮▮▮▮▮▮▮▮▮▮▮▮▮▮▮▮▮▮▮▮

▮▮▮▮▮▮ of my love for you, ▮▮▮▮▮▮▮▮▮▮▮▮▮▮

▮▮▮▮▮▮▮ of the fluorescent ▮▮▮▮▮▮▮▮▮▮▮▮

▮▮▮▮▮▮▮ of the secrecy ▮▮▮▮▮▮▮▮▮▮▮▮▮▮

▮▮▮ hard to ▮▮▮▮▮▮▮▮▮▮▮ be ▮▮▮▮▮▮ still

▮▮ solemn ▮▮▮▮▮▮▮▮▮▮▮▮▮▮▮▮▮▮▮▮▮▮▮▮▮

▮▮▮▮▮▮▮▮▮▮▮▮▮▮▮▮▮▮▮▮▮ drifting back and forth

▮▮▮▮▮▮▮▮▮ like a tree breathing ▮▮▮▮▮▮▮▮▮

▮▮▮▮▮▮▮▮▮▮▮▮▮▮▮▮▮▮▮▮▮▮▮▮▮▮▮▮▮▮▮

▮▮▮▮▮▮▮▮▮▮▮▮▮▮▮▮▮▮▮▮▮▮▮▮▮▮▮▮▮

                                        I look

at ▮▮▮▮▮▮▮▮▮▮▮▮▮▮▮▮▮▮▮▮▮▮▮▮▮▮▮▮▮

▮▮▮▮▮▮▮▮▮▮▮▮▮▮▮▮▮▮▮▮▮▮▮▮▮ the ▮▮▮

▮▮▮▮▮▮ heavens ▮▮▮▮▮▮▮▮▮▮▮▮▮▮▮▮▮▮▮▮

▮▮▮▮▮▮▮▮▮▮▮▮▮▮▮▮▮▮▮▮▮▮▮▮▮▮▮▮▮▮

▮▮▮▮▮▮▮▮▮ I never ▮▮▮▮▮▮▮▮▮▮▮▮▮▮▮▮▮

▮▮▮▮▮▮▮▮▮▮▮▮▮▮▮▮▮▮▮▮▮▮▮▮▮▮▮▮▮▮

▮▮▮▮▮▮▮▮▮▮▮▮▮▮▮▮▮▮▮▮▮▮▮▮▮▮▮▮▮

when ▮▮▮▮▮ got ▮▮ right ▮▮▮▮▮▮▮▮▮▮▮▮▮▮

▮▮▮▮▮▮▮▮▮▮▮▮▮▮▮▮▮▮▮▮▮▮▮▮▮▮▮▮▮▮

▮▮▮▮▮▮

▮▮▮▮▮▮▮▮▮▮▮▮▮▮▮▮▮▮▮▮▮▮▮▮▮▮▮▮▮▮

▮▮▮▮▮▮▮▮▮▮▮▮ wasted on me ▮▮▮▮▮▮▮▮▮▮

sick to my stomach on the

secrecy take people

hard to believe there can be anything as

solemn right in front of

the drifting

breathing

why in the world did

look

you look at all the

possibly anyway

thank heavens you

never

got the right person to stand near

BUILDING J

I don't know why I'm crying. Maybe it's because had I known last time was the last time, I might have done something different. I might have hugged you again, smelling like liquor. I might have held your hands. Held your potential here. Between mine. Instead, on those slabs of steps, the apartments where I lost things, we left each other. Scrapes in linoleum, dragging the fridge you took. Stain on the floor, your body overdosing. Finally, tubes in your veins and I doubted you. Because sometimes medicines don't mix. You shouldn't have been mixing them like that. It was a god complex, or perhaps you had nothing. So, you had nothing left to lose.

THE SUBTLE WAYS

I shrink myself. Wilting flower
stem spine curled up and in,
like when my backpack
was so heavy, a shell
for all my preciousness inside.

My body
leans forward,
apologizing for itself.
Speaks for me by rote.

Teach my ribcage to reach
downward, the fearful,
fluttering thing.

I HATE SCRATCHY BLANKETS AND COLD SKIN

Solace in that audible clock at night
Shoulders found a home nestled by my ears
The far wall of the room I brought home with me

Up to my bunk bed, littered with eyelashes
Stacked books, dead flashlights and keepsake boxes
Control

And now? I hate small talk
My eyelashes try
but they fall out on their own

II. MYCELIUM HEART

PRUNE

In cutting these ties
I feel like less

not cut like a freed balloon
but in the way I imagine

a house plant feels ready
open and raw

after someone who loves it snips off the dead things

less me
in the way of me
growing

SLEEPY ORANGE COUNTY SUBURBS IN
THE EARLY MORNING

There are no sweet spots
here, nothing that is ours.
Only model homes, freeways

marketplaces
too many streetlamps to see the moon.
At night the lights are too big for our eyes. Six lenses

between the two of us,
squinting watercolors.
In the car I cry,

the moon grows legs.
If we stay
idle long enough, the city glitters.

REPRISE

Thoughts swivel back around

click, ding.

Without clutching expectation
Hands free of heavy luggage, of wringing one another
Love held in tumbles out
Gratitude settles like a lake
My river mouth, wet with potential and truth
An ink pot for storytelling, lesson learning
My spine the quill and the paper
Scratching my way forward with a guess, winding in prayer
You be the typewriter, I'll be letters
bind me together for authenticity's sake

click, ding.

SOUTHERN CALIFORNIA DOESN'T HAVE WINTER

It just feels like summer gets sad. Green trees endure, some turn brown. Wait to shed crisp leaves, scatter them in parking lots. Chilly mornings, chilly evenings. Heavy sweaters stay in closets for vacations. Nice, comfortable. Few days are blustery, rainy even, but never for long.

The warmth stays. Same way my grief is a constant thing. Sadly comforting thing. Static underneath. Like when I turn the fan off in the morning to hear its absence. Like when the auditory hallucination stops suddenly and the silence roars. Southern California is always warm and I am lonely all the time.

SCORPIO'S FORGIVENESS

I know why you couldn't love me, but that doesn't let you off the hook.
You're still a piece of shit.

SECOND HAND

It will always be odd, time passing
I smell old clothes and feel my heart tug
I donate tiny sneakers that no longer fit on little feet
They go next to pots and pans that seasons wore slowly
The box feels fuller than it is
The moon grows and disappears
My dogs' beards grow lighter, and I cry

I AM OPENING

When I was a kid, we got a caterpillar kit with a big net enclosure. My siblings searched for perfect sticks and leaves so tiny, fuzzy bodies could make chrysalis homes. The shells grew bigger and sturdier until they didn't. We waited. Kept them in the darkest hallway. Coolest, safest place in our hectic little home.

I pulled my brother back when he'd press his nose too close. Imagining how horrifying it would be. To crash down in the middle of reshaping oneself, in the middle of healing. One day, one at a time, our caterpillars cracked through. It was messier than we thought it would be. Metamorphosis usually is. Dripping, skinny legs crawled through the slits. They sat. We watched as blood filled their wings. Covered in sticky red goo. They unfurled. Wings ten times bigger than their bodies in their boundless potential. We let them go.

They already knew how to fly. How lovely for them to wake up knowing that what they were yesterday would not keep them from where they wanted to go today.

REMEMBER WHEN THE TRAIL WAS ON FIRE?

I could taste smoke from two towns over
Flames chewed on hills for days
Now spaces
Between the big houses
Are riddled with ash piles
Singed patches
Of plant skeletons
The cacti came back so fast

Some trees are still scorched
I wonder
If they feel reborn

Gray ghosts with crisp, broken trunks
Grow plateaus of mushrooms. Bright orange staircases
Up to spiderwebs so thick they look like cotton candy
Spun fervent
Through cracks in the wood
Layered meticulously
Tiny architects wound whole leaves
Through them, built a strong enough foundation
To hold entire branches within
The burnt trees live

CRYPTKEEPING

Inside my tomb mind, a glut of thoughts once killed or loved
Past selves set down sweetly
they fell away
Saccharine innocence pooled at my feet
lifeless leaves at harvest

Others ripped off, flung inside, chest heaved triumphant
Contented to have peeled myself away, breathe deeply again
More still, without shape. Shreds
mangled by claws, gnashed by teeth desperate
to escape a self hellbent on ruin

Gravestones, mausoleum doors
lay a kiss on each
Lips cold through the empty corridor
crypt of endings
Glowing with nostalgia and never looking back

ACKNOWLEDGEMENTS

Thanks, now and always, to my little family. For foundation and cheerleading and everything in between, I could not have done this without you. I love you more than anything.

Thanks to my editor Matthew Feinstein for helping me tell my story. Thanks to The Poetry Lab for the spaces, lessons and encouragement that made many of these poems possible.

Sincerest thanks to *Nightingale & Sparrow Press* for featuring "Scorpio's Forgiveness" and to *Beyond The Veil Press* for publishing earlier versions of "Hell Can Be Anyone" and "Cryptkeeping".

Thank you, reader, the unsung hero of poetry. We can write all day, but the magic of poetry is when it finds a home in a reader's heart.

Finally, thank you to poets everywhere. The world needs your bravery and vulnerability, now and always.

ABOUT THE AUTHOR

Jessica June Cato is a writer, poet, and Editorial Fellow at The Poetry Lab, a community learning space for creative writers. Her work has been published by *Nightingale & Sparrow*, *Sampaguita Press* and *Chicanx Writers and Artist's Association*. Her favorite things include making memes, writing workshops, Nintendo switch, and her two small poodles.

You can find her on socials talking about Astrology For Poets, her series of articles, videos and workshop on astrology, poetry, and the ways they intertwine.

IG/Tiktok: *@jessjunewrites*
Web: *jessjunewrites.com*

ABOUT THE PRESS

Beyond The Veil Press is a queer-owned indie publisher based in Colorado.

We began as a Kickstarter project by two SCAD graduates (Sarah Herrin & Josiah Callaway) in March 2021, with the goal to promote the healing power of poetry & art while lifting the veil from "scary" topics of mental health.

Since then, our team has grown to include AJ Wojtalik, Tyler Hurula, and Kris Kaila. (Visit our site to meet them!) We believe that by sharing our darkest stories, we find we are not alone.

We donate 10% of each anthology sale to a featured mental health nonprofit. Please see our mental health resources page on our website and on the following page.

beyondtheveilpress.com
IG: @beyondtheveilpress
FB: /beyondtheveilpress

THANK YOU FOR SUPPORTING SMALL BUSINESS!

MENTAL HEALTH RESOURCES we love

BOOKS

Permission to come home: reclaiming mental health as Asian Americans - Jenny Wang
The Pain We Carry: Healing from C-PTSD for People of Color - Natalie Gutierrez
Journey Through Trauma: Guide to Healing Repeated Trauma - Gretchen Schmelzer
The Deepest Well - Dr. Nadine Burke Harris
My Grandmother's Hands - Resmaa Menakem *tw: police violence*
What My Bones Know - Stephanie Foo (memoir)
The Journey From Abandonment To Healing – Susan Anderson
Waking The Tiger - Peter Levine
Polysecure: Attachment, Trauma, & Consensual Nonmonogamy – Jessica Fern
Self-Therapy: A Step-By-Step Guide to Healing Your Inner Child Using IFS - Jay Early
The Body Keeps The Score – Bessel van der Kolk *problematic but worth reading*

WEBSITES

activeminds.org - Mental health awareness and education for students.
afsp.org - Saving lives and bringing hope to those affected by suicide.
adaa.org - Anxiety & Depression Society of America
thetrevorproject.org - Crisis intervention and suicide prevention services for LGBTQ youth
RAINN.org - for survivors of sexual assault

PODCASTS

Where Is My Mind? – Niall Breslin
The Hilarious World of Depression; Depreche Mode – John Moe
The Happiness Lab – Dr. Laurie Santos
Speaking of Psychology – Kim I. Mills
Being Well – Dr. Rick Hanson and Forrest Hanson
Sober Awkward - Hamish Adams-Cairns and Victoria Vanstone

OTHER TITLES BY BEYOND THE VEIL PRESS

2023

Anthology 4: *We Apologize For The Inconvenience* - Queer & Trans
    Voices to benefit Club Q
Maybe She's Born With It, Maybe It's Trauma by Cait Thomson
Surviving Peter Pan by Marissa Forbes
Anthology 5: *Do Not Tap On The Glass*
TRANSabdominal Retrieval by Teddy Goetz
We Are Creatures Of What Has Happened by Ashley Mezzano

Coming Soon:
Anthology 6: *Relics of Unbearable Softness* - Queer & Trans Voices
Neurotica For The Modern Doomscroller by Eddie Brophy

Anthology: Survivors of Sexual Assault (title TBD)
Anthology: Poets Of Color BIPOC (title TBD)

2022

Anthology 2: Tea With My Monster
Heretic: A Story of Spiritual Liberation in Poems by Kristy Webster
Anti/Muse Adult Coloring Book
Anti/Muse Lined Notebooks
Anthology 3: *How To Heal A Bloodline*

2021

Anthology 1: *There Is A Monster Inside That I Am Learning To Love*
Anti/Muse: Poems by Sarah Herrin & Illustrations by Josiah Callaway

Made in the USA
Middletown, DE
22 September 2023

39033109R00031